# TAUNTON
## IN OLD PHOTOGRAPHS

ONE OF THE LAST PHOTOGRAPHS to be added to the collection. Preliminary research suggests that this is the shop of Charles Allen at No. 19 East Reach. The last occupier of this building was G.H. Pike (baker) before it was demolished in around 1930 to widen the entrance to Eastbourne Road. Can any reader confirm this? (Photograph by W. Crockett.)

# TAUNTON
## IN OLD PHOTOGRAPHS

COLLECTED BY

## NICK CHIPCHASE

ALAN SUTTON
1989

Alan Sutton Publishing
Gloucester

First published 1989

**British Library Cataloguing in Publication Data**

Taunton in old photographs.
1. Somerset. Taunton, history
I. Chipchase, Nick
942.3'87

ISBN 0-86299-645-7

Front Cover Illustration:

PARADE MARKET DAY in the early 1880s. Gas lamps are still in evidence. Henry Massingham's
first permanent electric light installation on the Parade was inaugurated officially on 1 May
1886.

Typesetting and origination by
Alan Sutton Publishing
Printed in Great Britain by
Dotesios Printers Limited

# CONTENTS

# INTRODUCTION

The aim of this book is to illustrate pictorially the changes that have taken place in the town of Taunton during the past 120 years. The period covered by the majority of the photographs which appear in the book date between 1900 and 1935. The first decades of the century were ones of slow but continuous change; recent years have seen a further acceleration of change and wholesale redevelopment, resulting in a Taunton today that is far removed from the town of 1900.

The town has always been an important centre of communications, being situated geographically in the centre of the south west penninsula. River, canal, rail and road links have played an important role in the development of the town and its industries.

In the 1930s these industries were many and diversified but so unobtrusive that visitors from the industrial areas of the North would scarcely recognize their existence. In 1936 there were five shirt and collar factories, gloves and silks were also important industries, while blouses, pyjamas and leggings completed the range of clothing which Taunton helped supply to the world. Engineering absorbed a considerable amount of male labour, high-speed steam-engines, mortar mills, etc. being exported all over the world by Messrs Easton and Johnson Ltd. The Great Western Railway also had extensive engineering shops and concrete works employing many hundreds of men. The manufacture of paper, cider and fruit products, church organs, motor car bodies, dairy products, brewing and malting was also carried on in factories in the borough or adjacent areas.

As a commercial and shopping centre Taunton remains important. Fifty years ago the town was the recognized commercial centre for Somerset; government departments, banks, insurance companies, etc. all having their district offices in the town, while county administration, Quarter Sessions and Assizes, traffic commissioners and meetings of all important bodies in Somerset were (and in many cases still are) centred at Taunton.

Lying in the fertile vale of Taunton Deane, with beautiful surrounding country, Taunton also commends itself as a residential, touring and agricultural centre. The market has been important for centuries and, although previously held within the town, it is now held in the former Jarvis Field adjacent to the river. Continuing commercial pressures deem it likely that the market will, in future, move yet again to a larger site further out of town. Prior to 1930, cattle, sheep, horses, calves and pigs were sold on Castle Green every Saturday between 9 a.m. and 4 p.m. During the same day corn and hops were sold at the Corn Exchange and there were covered markets for butchers, poultry dealers and fishmongers. An open market was held on the Parade where local produce and wares were sold from temporary stalls.

Hunting in the Deane has long been a popular pastime among the local community. At one time six local packs operated in the area. Two of these, Taunton Vale Harriers and Taunton Vale Foxhounds, had kennels near the town. Other leisure and sporting pursuits were catered for by nearly 100 acres of playing fields and recreation grounds, plus grounds for cricket, rugby and football (1936).

Taunton Racecourse, just outside of town, one mile and three furlongs round, is an important venue for race-meetings. Other well catered for activities included; bowling, golf, polo and swimming. A motor cycle and light car club operated in the town. Important annual events included the Taunton Dog Show, The Taunton and West of England Horse Show and the still important Horticultural Show in Vivary Park. Taunton has a long tradition as an important educational and ecclesiastical centre. Between the wars some 20 churches, chapels and halls served Baptist, Church of England, Congregational, Plymouth Brethren, Quaker, Roman Catholic, Salvation Army, Unitarian and Wesleyan Methodist congregations.

A local guide of 1907 refers thus to the educational establishments in the town – 'A classic fragrance pervades the town and neighbourhood whose colleges and schools were never so actively engaged as now. The variety of the establishments, considering the size of the town, is simply astonishing. Their reputation is more than National.' Certainly then, as now, the large colleges and schools around the town have played an important part in the education of British and foreign students alike. Taunton was formerly an important military town being once the depot for the 13th Prince Albert's Light Infantry, better known as the Somerset Light Infantry. The achievements of the Somerset Regulars, Militia, Volunteers and Yeomanry are well documented in a fine Military Museum. The Burmese Memorial and Jellalabad Barracks are also testimony to Somerset men serving in foreign parts. Apart from the Military Museum, Taunton Castle is also home to the County museum and Somerset Archaeological and Natural History Society Collections; the Castle having been acquired by the Society in 1874.

A brief description of the town should not omit to mention the river from whence it derives its name – the River Tone. This rises in the Brendon Hills some 15 miles from Taunton and joins the Parrett at Burrowbridge. Below Taunton the river and canal served as important commercial routes prior to the railways. Later the river served the breweries, foundries and mills situated along its banks. Nowadays its commercial value is minimal but it does enhance the gardens, walks and parks in the town.

Hopefully a flavour of all of these, and the changes that have occurred over the last 50 years are reflected by the photographs in this book. I have concentrated on the 1900–1935 era as I believe this will be within the living memory of many local inhabitants.

The earlier photographs in the book come from cartes-de-visites and photographs produced by the 20 or so commercial photographers operating in the town prior to 1900. Of these, John Chaffin (from c. 1883), W.A. Crockett (from c. 1895), A. Petherick (from c. 1872) and Henry Montague Cooper were most prominent. Montague Cooper's photographic business in Taunton spanned nearly 40 years. His work covered the entire county of Somerset and was extensively used in town guides, pamphlets, etc. His output of postcards was probably the largest in Somerset. Montague Cooper succeeded to the business of W. Morley in around 1890 and he married Jenny (a Catholic), Morley's daughter. She lived in a cottage in Park Street and they were probably married at St George's Church.

By 1915 Montague Cooper had shops at Taunton, Chard, Wellington, Burnham-On-Sea, Bridgwater and Lynton. At the Taunton shop a large staff was employed including Frenchmen and Belgians. Jenny was particularly talented in photography and did much of the artistic work in the developing and printing side of the business. During the First World War Taunton was home to Australia's Siege Batteries and the soldiers were particularly keen to send home pictures of snow scenes. When the weather did not oblige, Jenny faked the photographs by flicking solution onto the negatives with a toothbrush. To prove their ability with processing the juniors had to 'remove' the buttons on a soldier's uniform by carefully retouching the photographs.

Initially Montague Cooper travelled the county in a horse-drawn waggon advertising Kodak film. Not long after 1900 a 3½ hp Benz car was acquired and during the First World War he was one of the first people in Taunton to power his car with a gasbag on the roof. The shop in East Street, Taunton, had a long aisle which ran through to Magdalen Street. There were two dressing rooms, a darkroom and two artist rooms, a studio and reception room. At the time of the First World War carbon arc lights and a large diffusing screen were used for studio portraits. Natural daylight was also extensively used. The glass negatives were stored in the cellar. Bundles of these were wrapped in oiled paper and carefully catalogued. A serious fire in around 1921 damaged the shop and equipment but the negatives were saved. A temporary studio was used on the other side of the street and the negatives moved to a cottage in Tancred Street.

The Montague Coopers lived over the shop, they had no children, the nearest relatives being two nieces. In around 1930 the couple retired and moved to Torquay. Most of the shops were offered to the resident managers, Wellington being the last to be sold. The valuable glass negative collection comprising many thousands was sold to Miss Philips (a Taunton employee of 15 years) for the nominal fee of half a crown. Her father, rather unsure of where to store this bulky collection, tried in vain to get them housed in several of the larger schools in the town. Unfortunately nobody had the foresight to appreciate the value of such a collection and all the negatives were eventually destroyed. Considering the scope and extent of Montague Cooper's work (one of his assignments was to record the 73 public houses owned by Starkey Knight and Ford), an archival record of immense value was forever lost.

From 1900–1914 the popularity of the postcard as a form of communication was enormous and the majority of illustrations in this book are from this source. Over 50 local and 80 national publishers produced postcards of the town over the years. The full range and extent of these cards can only be guessed at, but the numbers must run into a figure in excess of 5,000. Many are the popular views of prominent streets and buildings, just occasionally, however, a 'gem' will be found, showing such diverse views as; the gasworks, the prison or railway station, or featuring some special event or disaster. Local schools produced views of school life and many small shops and industries issued postcards advertising their wares or services. Cards such as these are treasure to the student of local history.

In conclusion, I would wish to say that I hope the reader has obtained some small pleasure from looking back over an ever-changing town and social conditions. Also perhaps, to reflect that sometimes material improvements and 'progress' have not always brought us to the position where we can look back 80 years and say 'isn't life a lot better now'.

Nick Chipchase 1989

# SECTION ONE

# Streets and Highways

CENTRAL TAUNTON FROM THE AIR c. 1927. The Market House, top centre, still has the arcades each side, these were demolished in 1930. The Castle Green area is laid out for the cattle and sheep market which moved to its present site in 1929. (Aerofilms)

HIGH STREET c. 1902. A photograph taken from near the park gates. The window on the extreme right bears the words 'Soldiers Home', which was opened on 10 February 1902 by Miss Emily Weston at the former Rose and Crown Inn. (H.C. Colman)

HIGH STREET c. 1905. To the left is the Devon and Somerset Stores. Their proud boast of 'Over 10,000 articles sold' adorns the wall. Locally the shop was known only as 'The Stores', they also had a branch at Exeter. (Senior)

FORE STREET c. 1902. The 'Tudor House' is the oldest surviving domestic building in Taunton, the main structure dating from the fourteenth century. The initials 'T.T.' and 'I.T.' with the date 1578 on the frontage are those of Thomas (died 1620) and Joan Trowbridge who held the premises around that time. In later years, from 1871–1906, Charles Lewis (West Somerset Stores) occupied the site. From 1909–1946 the building housed Halliday's antique shop.

FORE STREET, LOOKING EAST, C. 1930. The premises left to right are: Taplin, baker; S. Hilton's Bootmaker's; Barnicott and Pearce the Printer's; Thelma the Tobacconist's and the Home and Colonial Stores.

FORE STREET, LOOKING WEST, C. 1904. Fisher and Sons' double frontage occupies the centre of the picture. The shop was described thus in the 1890s: 'The shop fronts are solid and business-like yet withal handsome and attractive.' (see page 45 for a closer view). (Stewart and Wolf)

FORE STREET c. 1905. The Market House is on the left. Also in view are the market arcades which were demolished in 1930. (J.M.J)

A LATER VIEW OF FORE STREET, c. 1925. Not much time to stand in the road now that motor traffic has increased. This time the actions of the photographer are of far less notice. (Frith)

FORE STREET C. 1914, looking towards the Market House. To the left is Marshalsea's Garage. Clements and Brown (right) greatly extended their store in 1907 by incorporating three shops into one. (W.H.S. Grosvenor R.P.)

EAST STREET c. 1902. Double decker tram No. 1 passes the London Hotel horse bus. The two ladies (left) are peering into John Chaffin, the photographer's, shop window. The shop canopy supports were ideal for tethering horses or propping up cycles. (Frith)

EAST STREET, as above but a later view taken in 1929 by the Francis Frith Company. Chaffin's shop has now been incorporated into the hotel which had its name changed to The County Hotel in 1919.

TAUNTON, EAST STREET

EAST STREET C. 1914. Montague Cooper's photography studio (Acacia House) is on the extreme right. The tramlines and overhead supply cables are clearly visible in this view. (W.H.S. Grosvenor RP)

EAST STREET C. 1933. To the right is the County Hotel and beyond this Steeven's Furnishing Store, the business was established in 1836. Mr Brunt's well-known tobacconist's shop is on the left. The tramway-standards have been converted to telegraph poles. (J.M.J.)

FORE STREET FROM EAST STREET, C. 1915. W.J. Coles were saddle and harness makers between c. 1906 and 1931. After this date they converted the shop to a fancy goods dealers. (Lilywhite)

EAST STREET c. 1902 with a tram passing-loop in the foreground. The man up the ladder is servicing an arc lamp. Frequent inspections of the lamps were required to clean the insides of the globes. (Wrench)

EAST STREET c. 1907. The Old Council House (centre) had formerly accommodated the offices of the Local Board of Health until it was absorbed by the new Taunton Corporation in 1877. The Corporation also met there until the purchase of the present Municipal Buildings in 1887.

EAST REACH C. 1902. The granite drinking fountain erected in 1860 (left) is now in Vivary Park. The premises behind this belonged to Mr G. Paul, the well-known pawnbroker. ('Georgie Paul's three brass balls') (M. Cooper)

EAST REACH, C. 1902. The Taunton and Somerset Hospital (left) was opened for patients in March 1812 to celebrate the Jubilee of George III. The Nursing Institute was built next to the hospital to commemorate the Jubilee of Queen Victoria 1887. (Tuck)

THE END OF EAST REACH and the gatehouse at Leycroft. St Margaret's Hospital (the Old Leper House) can be seen in the distance. At this time, c. 1900, Browning the butcher's shop adjoined the building. This later became W.P. Edwards Motor and Cycle shop (see p. 53) and a general grocery before it was demolished in around 1930. (Brice)

Park Street and St. John's Church, Taunton.

PARK STREET c. 1904 and St John's Church. One would expect it to be difficult to herd cows along this busy street today. (Stengel)

THE PARADE AND KINGLAKE MEMORIAL C. 1908. G. Small and Sons' coal delivery cart is passing the Corn Exchange. The Kinglake Memorial was erected in 1867 and removed in 1934. The large building in the centre is the Victoria Rooms built as the new market in 1821 and demolished in 1963. This housed the meat and vegetable market until 1929, and a British Restaurant during the Second World War. The Corn Exchange opened as the fish market in April 1854 and was demolished in 1937. (W.A. Crockett)

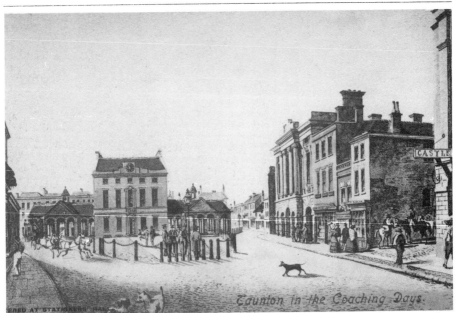

TAUNTON IN THE COACHING DAYS C. 1829. The Market House was built in 1770 on a site that had previously been cleared of houses etc. The Parade provided a focal point for the centre of town and it was here that a twice weekly market was held until 1929. (E. Goodman)

THE PARADE AND MARKET HOUSE C. 1908. In this view the arc lamp in front of the Kinglake Memorial can plainly be seen. To celebrate the centenary of permanent electric lighting in Taunton the Council erected a replica lamp in the same position in 1986. (E.J. Lamb)

FORE STREET FROM CORPORATION STREET *c.* 1929. This view clearly shows the end of the old market arcades which were removed in 1930. (W.H.S. Kingsway)

CORPORATION STREET *c.* 1910, showing the Library and School of Art buildings. To the extreme left is C. Lock's Borough Motor and Cycle Depot. The street was built through the gardens of the Old Grammar School in 1893–94. (Boots)

THE CRESCENT c. 1905, showing the south end near the junction with Upper High Street. (Frith)

THE CRESCENT c. 1905, the north end, a view taken near the junction with Park Street. The peacocks were removed from the Crescent Fields (right) in 1907 after complaints about the noise they made. County Hall was built here in 1935. (W.A. Crockett)

TAUNTON, NORTH STREET

NORTH STREET c. 1914. A.E. de Breffe, a former employee of Taunton furnishers Lawrence and Thompson, had opened his own antique furniture shop in the old Nag's Head building early in 1912. Here de Breffe is moving the business to Fore Street and the Midland Bank are preparing to take over the premises. The National Provincial Bank (centre) opened its own new building for business on 19 March 1912 after moving from No. 21 Fore Street. The cart in this view belongs to Goodlands the coal merchants. (Grosvenor RP)

NORTH STREET C. 1928, showing the refreshment kiosk (right) which served the Parade Market prior to 1929. (W.H.S.)

NORTH STREET 1912. On the left attached to E. Goodman's shop is the Goss sign advertising the sole Taunton agency of W.H. Goss for the sale of – 'miniature china pieces emblazoned with the Borough Arms (new and old), The Corporation Seal and a variety of other devices.' (Frith)

NORTH STREET c. 1902. A boy endeavours to control a frisky calf in front of the Castle Hotel portico. The odd looking cart on the right is S.J. Wright and Company's UCV Creamery milk delivery cart. (Chapman)

NORTH STREET, a later view to that above, taken by the Frith Company in 1912. The National Provincial Bank, extreme right, replaced the old Nos. 50 and 51 North Street in 1912.

TONE BRIDGE, c. 1914. The large building on the right housed Mr Trood's potato and manure warehouse and H. Corner and Company's woollen manufactory. (W.H.S. Grosvenor RP)

TONE BRIDGE, a later view dating c. 1925. By this time Allen's premises had been remodelled and Deller's Cafe opened.

THE BRIDGE c. 1919. The building on the left adjacent to the river has housed; the West of England Boot and Shoe Supply Company owned by Henry Massingham until c. 1900, Belben Bros. Hardware Store until c. 1915, Mettam and Lewis Athletic Outfitters until c. 1936 and Webber's Sports. Throughout this time the Singer Shop opposite has remained the same. (E.A. Pickard)

THE BRIDGE c. 1925, a slightly later view than the previous one. Although the tramlines have gone the poles still remain.

Bridge Street. Taunton. ℝ 38358

BRIDGE STREET C. 1907. There is plenty of interesting detail in a photograph such as this. On the extreme left is the Telegraph Inn, the covered cart (centre) belongs to Mr G. Paul the well-known Taunton pawnbroker. Above this a sign advertises Pratt's Motor Spirit. The term 'petrol' was coined by Carless, Capel and Leonard and at this time they had exclusive rights to its use. (Stengel)

BRIDGE STREET c. 1912. Easily dated to before 1913 as the Lyceum at the end of the street has yet to be built. Winter's Ironmongers on the left became the Labour Exchange in later years before the building was finally demolished to widen Wood Street. (Valentine)

STATION ROAD, c. 1907. Premises right to left are: W. Webber's antique furniture shop; Baker's Commercial Hotel; The Ashton Hotel and Jerred Hann, Stone and Marble Masons. (Stengel)

HAMMET STREET C. 1800. Before this street was built in 1788 the area on all sides of St Mary's was said to consist of 'alleys containing houses of the worst description, the homes of the bullies, thieves, drunkards and prostitutes who disgraced the town.' (Goodman)

HAMMET STREET in the 1920s. This is rather a rare view of the street, as most photographers seem to have preferred a view uncluttered with people and traffic.

ALFRED STREET C. 1905. A splendid rare view of this street with Somerset Place at the bottom left. The fine railings on either side have long since disappeared. (W.A. Crockett)

THE AVENUE C. 1905. Built as one of Taunton's more refined streets to house the 'better off'. (Brice)

CANN STREET from the air probably in the 1920s before the street was widened by the demolition of all the buildings on the right-hand side. Also in view is Westgate Street, Shuttern (before widening), St John's Church, the Shire Hall, Crescent and gasworks. (Photochrom Co.)

ST AUGUSTINE STREET NORTH, C. 1907, looking towards Van Trump's clothing factory. This end of the street had only recently been built and ended at the factory. Priory Bridge Road, now running along the bottom, did not open until 1922. (Brice)

SOUTH ROAD LOOKING NORTH, C. 1910. The road into Taunton from the south-east near the old town boundary. This area of road had the odd name of Cuckoo Corner. (Chapman)

HOLWAY ROAD NEAR HOLWAY BRIDGE, C. 1910. A companion view to that above, again near the old town boundary. Trinity Church can be seen to the right. (Chapman)

GEORGE STREET C. 1907. One of Taunton's quieter streets, although the appearance of the photographer has attracted a small crowd. (Brice)

ST ANDREW'S ROAD C. 1908, recently the scene of extensive highway 'improvements'. On the left is W. Pearse's furniture store.

THE PARADE ON MARKET DAY, C. 1902. A policeman chats to a stall holder and a new electric tram stops to admit passengers. Hansom cabs ring the Parade. (M. Cooper)

THE PARADE MARKET C. 1923. Motor taxis first appeared in 1908 and the first taximeter to be used in Taunton was in 1917. The only horse transport to be seen is W.E. & T. Cousin's delivery cart on the left. This view contrasts well with that above of some twenty years earlier. (J.M.J.)

# SECTION TWO

# Commerce

THE LIVESTOCK MARKET, CASTLE GREEN, c. 1909. Cattle were sold in the area to the left while the sheep-pens were on the right. The market moved to its present site in 1929.

ALLEN AND SONS TONE BRIDGE FOUNDRY, c. 1910. The business originated as the Tone Bridge Iron and Brass Foundry in 1816. In later years Allen's became more concerned with the motor trade. (W. Pollard)

TAUNTON MOTOR RADIATOR WORKS in the 1920s, owned by Mr G.D. Laverock. This was situated at Mill Lane adjacent to North Street. Mr Laverock started his business in around 1919 and later ran it with his son until it closed in around 1954.

ALFRED BEARE'S DRAPERY SHOP at No. 9 North Street, c. 1907. A few years later Mr Beare moved his business across the road to a larger shop (at Nos. 43–44) specially designed to let in the maximum daylight.

SIBLEY AND THORNE'S DRAPERY STORE, c. 1906, at Nos. 4, 5 and 6 Eastgate. This postcard has been signed by J.P. Sibley who was Mayor of Taunton at this time.

MAYPOLE DAIRY COMPANY in 1916 at No. 33A Fore Street. The figure on the right was Charlie Boon later to become a motor driver. He lost his nerve for driving and after a period of unemployment cycled away from his brother's house at Rowbarton to drown himself in the canal.

THE MUSIC STORES c. 1914, No. 67 High Street. In the doorway stands Mr Clement Smith, the proprietor and his apprentice Albert Chubb later believed killed in action.

From **W. H. WESTLAKE & SON**,

Specialities
in
School
Suits,
Sports
Suits,
and
Complete
Outfits.

Inspection
Invited.

**Tailors and Outfitters, TAUNTON**

ADVERTISING POSTCARD FOR W.H. WESTLAKE & SON C. 1910. Westlake's had their Tailor's and Outfitter's shop in High Street.

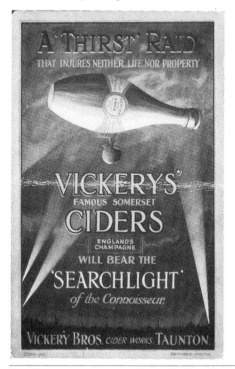

A 'THIRST' RAID
THAT INJURES NEITHER LIFE NOR PROPERTY

VICKERYS'
FAMOUS SOMERSET
CIDERS
ENGLAND'S
CHAMPAGNE
WILL BEAR THE
'SEARCHLIGHT'
of the Connoisseur.

VICKERY BROS. CIDER WORKS. TAUNTON.

ADVERTISING POSTCARD FOR VICKERY'S CIDER c. 1916, employing a topical First World War theme. Vickery Brother's West Somerset Cider Works were at Rowbarton from around 1911–1920. By 1923 they were egg merchants and proprietors of the Gaiety Cinema.

G. GRAVES GROCER AND MINERAL WATER MANUFACTURER, the shop in East Reach decorated for the 1911 coronation. George Graves came to Taunton from Hemyock and served his grocery apprenticeship with John Lee at No. 9 East Street. Mr Graves opened his own business at the Old Council House in East Street but moved to his East Reach premises in around 1895. When George Graves retired in 1923 his son Albert continued the business into the 1930s. George Graves died in March 1930, aged 62.

FISHER & SONS SHOP (part) at Nos. 8 and 9 Fore Street, c. 1910. The business was founded in around 1830 and during the latter part of the nineteenth century Fishers were known locally as 'The Grate People'. They traded as ironmongers and in later years employed staff to install and service heating systems.

GREGORY AND WRENN'S CHEMIST SHOP No. 15 East Street, c. 1910. The company had two Taunton shops with branches at Wellington and Langport. Mr W.A. Wrenn, who died in 1911, was twice Mayor of Taunton. He formed the partnership with Mr G.H. Gregory in 1885.

JACOB'S GENERAL FURNISHING WAREHOUSE shortly after its conversion from the White Hart Hotel in 1865. Adjacent to this is Mr R. Woollatt's chemist shop which moved across the road to No. 20 Fore Street in 1878.

THE DEVON AND SOMERSET STORES c. 1907, successor to Jacob's store above. The Stores, as it was known, traded for 100 years in Taunton and was one of the best known shops in the area. It sold practically every type of merchandise and was sadly missed when demolished in 1968. (Stengel)

REFRONTING CHAPMAN'S STORE, C. 1895. This store was also a popular shop trading in the town from 1864–1972 when Debenhams took over the site. It was founded by two London brothers, William and Arthur Chapman, 'for the sale of articles of sterling quality and value'. The *Gazette* of 7 March 1914 published an extensive Jubilee history of the Company.

BAKER AND LUDLOW'S BUTCHER'S SHOP at Upper High Street, c. 1908. Mr Baker stands in the doorway of the premises which were later demolished to widen the street.

R. PEARSE AND SONS IRONMONGER'S SHOP, c. 1907, at No. 31 Station Road. The window display features a fine array of lamps, bird cages, sieves, hand tools, buckets and baths. (SPT PPC)

OLIVER'S BOOT AND SHOE WAREHOUSE, c. 1910, at No. 4 Cheapside. At the time the photograph was taken the manager was Mr T. Gerry.

INTERIOR OF HALLIDAY'S ANTIQUE SHOP, c. 1915, inside the Tudor House. Hallidays took over the premises in 1909 when the West Somerset Stores vacated the site. (M. Cooper)

CHAPMAN'S STORE, NORTH STREET, C. 1930. An interesting episode occurred in the store in January 1900. Two gas engineers called to locate a gas leak did so in the obvious manner – with a light! The resulting explosion was said to have 'upset the equilibrium of the people in the room and relocate the staircase', one young lady also suffered a crushed hand. Further structural and stock damage occurred. It seems odd nobody thought it prudent to evacuate the store.

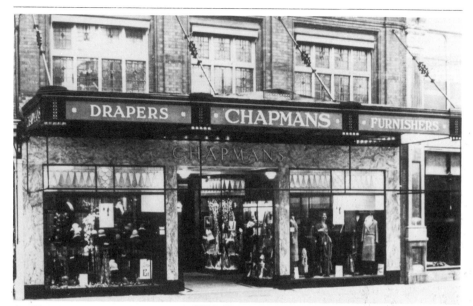

CHAPMAN'S STORE, CENTRE SECTION, C. 1930. The shop at this time was selling (in the decimal equivalent) – Tweed skirts at 50p, cotton frocks at £1.20, smart coats at £2.50 and klingsil hose stockings at 15p.

BINDON'S MILK DELIVERY CART, C. 1910. Josiah Bindon's East Reach Dairy was at No. 1 Victoria Street.

M. COOPER'S PHOTOGRAPHIC STUDIO, EAST STREET, c. 1907. Mr Cooper came to Taunton from his native Cheltenham aged seventeen, in around 1884. His first local job was as a salesman in a furnishing warehouse, he later became one of Taunton's best known photographers and pioneer motorists.

CHARLES LOCK'S PARK CYCLE DEPOT, c. 1910, at Upper High Street. Mr Lock also ran the Borough Cycle Works in Corporation Street.

# SECTION THREE

# Transport

W.P. EDWARDS' CYCLE SHOP, C. 1908. This adjoined the old Leper Hospital. Mr C. Webber is seen seated on an unusual machine known as a forecar. Mr Edwards also had a shop in Corporation Street and claimed to have sold the first motor cycle in Taunton. The Taunton and District Motor Cycle Club had their opening run to Burnham-On-Sea in May 1911. Their first captain was Thomas Crump (see page 54).

*London Hotel. Taunton.*
*Proprietor, E. H. Claridge.*
*Head-Quarters of the Automobile Club.*
*'Phone. 0134.*

FRENCH AUTOMOBILISTS sponsored by the De Dion Bouton Motor Company. Seen here on 21 July 1904 on a visit to the newly formed Somerset Automobile Club. De Dion based machines were being offered for sale by the Bridgwater Motor Company in 1901. The cost of the machine included free driving tuition. The man on the tricycle is Tom Crump, a Taunton character, surveyor to the Rural District Council and pioneer motor-cyclist. (M. Cooper)

CHARLES LOCK'S PARK CYCLE DEPOT decorated for the 1911 coronation of King George V. The motor cycle on the right is a V-twin Rex with an unusual form of front fork springing and wicker side chair.

TAUNTON MOTOR COMPANY'S CHARABANC 'SOMERSET LASS', c. 1914. In April 1914 she was running local folk to Blue Ball (Wills Neck), Sidmouth, Wincanton Races and Burnham-On-Sea. In September the same year, along with other local charabancs, she had a truck body fitted, was marked 'WD' and sent to Southampton for the war effort.

C.H. BAILEY'S CYCLE SHOP in 1898 at No. 52 Bridge Street. Cycling was a popular late Victorian pastime. Henry Van Trump was a founder member of the Taunton Bicycle Club formed in August 1877. Several local cycle shop proprietors progressed to motor cycles and cars in the early 1900s.

HOLT TRACTOR and First World War transport at Rowbarton Recreation Ground, c. 1916. The Holt, an American agricultural tractor, was obtained for use as a heavy artillery tractor but also served as the inspiration for the trials vehicles that led eventually to the tank. (M. Cooper)

HOWITZER DRAWN BY HOLT TRACTOR in East Reach, c. 1916. Originally six inch naval guns, these howitzers were rebored to eight inches and mounted on traction engine wheels. Much of this work was done at various railway engineering depots. (M. Cooper)

CHAPMAN'S LEYLAND MOTOR DELIVERY VAN registered 13 March 1922. Chapman's were among the first local companies to use motor vehicles for delivery purposes. Earlier transport included traction engines and steam lorries.

CHAPMAN'S MOTOR VAN IN A DITCH 1921. Circumstances of the accident are unknown but the vehicle is another Leyland.

JAMES BEACH'S STEAM WAGONETTE c. 1900. In April 1900 Mr Beach was offering to build or supply oil, steam or electric cars to any design. These were built at his Pioneer Motor Car and Engineering Works established in 1873. The steam 'car' was built to a design that was inspired by a four foot long model made by Mr Beach's two sons. It is probable James Beach built the first mechanically propelled road vehicle manufactured in Taunton. Mr Beach's daughter, Daisy, was the first Taunton woman to drive a car in 1901, at the age of fourteen. In later years Mr Beach developed an interest in aeroplanes but it is not known how many, if any, he built. (An advert of 1911 refers to Beach and Sons Motor and Aeroplane Works).

THE LONDON HOTEL MOTOR BUS, c. 1914, built by Marshalsea of Ilminster on a Napier chassis. Seating ten persons inside and one out, she had her inaugural run to Ilminster and back early in 1914. Her coachwork was dark blue with matching upholstery. (Grosvenor RP)

CHAPMAN'S HORSE-DRAWN HEARSE c. 1907. The last ride for many a Tauntonian.

THE KLONDYKE HORSE BUS on its first run in January 1898. This was introduced by John Elston, the proprietor of the Parade Hotel (formerly the Bristol Arms). The bearded gentleman, seated top centre, appears to be the artist Harry Frier who died in the workhouse in 1921. The Nag's Head closed in 1911.

G. WEST AND SONS' LORRY, first registered by Mr West on 15 December 1919. This vehicle was a Lacre O-type introduced in 1909. It was powered by a four-cylinder thirty horsepower petrol engine. A three-speed gearbox drove the rear axle via two chains.

THE MOTOR BUS 'LADY BETTY' in Corporation Street, c. 1914. The bus was acquired second-hand by Allen's of Taunton for Mr Ireland, the well-known carrier between Churchstanton and Taunton. Her first run was to Stapley for Mr Ireland's inspection in May 1914. After touring the area with friends, Mr Ireland returned to Stapley to a triumphal arch and other decorations with the display of words 'Success to the car' and 'Ireland for ever'. She was probably the earliest local out-of-town motor bus service and ran until 1920.

MOTOR TRAFFIC outside White's and the Crown Hotels, High Street, 1925. These three vehicles are; a Wolseley, a Morris Oxford and a Ford Model-T truck. Morris' Oxford and Cowley range were some of the best selling cars of the time. In 1925, 54,151 of these were built comprising 41 per cent of new car production in Britain. The famous Model-T Ford was 'the car that put the world on wheels'. Some 16.5 million were built between 1908 and 1927. (Frith)

# The Tramway

A DOUBLE-DECKED TRAM WITH CREW C. 1902. 'I've a zeed 'em goo by hosses, I've a zeed 'em goo by steam but be dazzed it ever I've azeed 'em goo by vishing rods avore.'

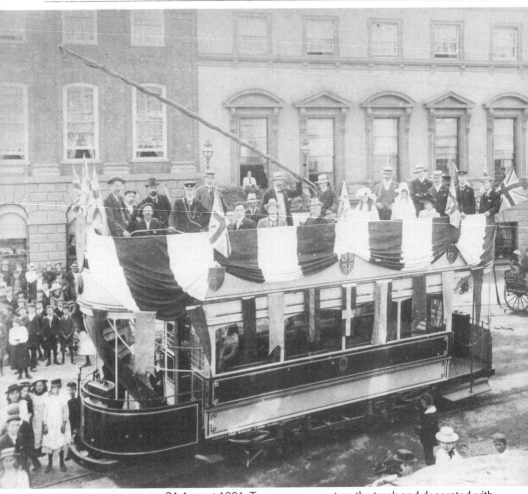

FIRST TAUNTON TRAM RUN, 21 August 1901. Two cars were put on the track and decorated with flags and banners by W. & A. Chapman Limited. The first run began at 5 p.m. and during the evening 2,000 people rode in the cars. (Souvenir photograph by Montague Cooper)

DOUBLE-DECKED TRAM IN STATION ROAD, 1902. The elaborate tramway-standard can plainly be seen. After the closure of the system in 1921 some standards were converted to lamp-standards and a few still remain in Greenway Crescent.

A CLOSER VIEW OF THE DOUBLE-DECKED TRAM, c. 1902. The original fleet consisted of six double-decked four wheelers built and supplied by the Brush Company. Seating capacity totalled 50 passengers, 26 outside and 24 inside.

DISMANTLING THE DOUBLE-DECKERS at the depot in 1905. The system was closed for eight weeks in 1905 while the tracks were relaid on granite setts and six new single-deck cars introduced. The old cars were sold to the Leamington and Warwick Electrical Company Limited, where some of them survived until the system closed in 1930.

MR W. SMITH, manager of the tram depot stands proudly at the helm of the new single-decker just delivered by the Brush Company in 1905. By this time it had been realised that no further extensions to the system were likely and that this type of car would meet the public demand.

NUMBER SIX in the early years of service, C. 1908, running along North Street. The seating capacity of these cars was 24 and they had a strong American flavour with the glass ventilated clerestory roofs above four side windows.

ENTRANCE TO THE TRAMWAY DEPOT, c. 1910. The line into the depot was the sharpest curve in the system. It entered a narrow unmade lane at the turning after Alfred Street. At the shed (measuring 120ft × 35ft) the line fanned out into three roads. (Chapman)

SINGLE-DECKER IN FORE STREET, with the town possibly decorated for the 1911 coronation. The posters advertise Taunton Horse and Dog Shows. (M. Cooper)

THE TRAMWAY STAFF, C. 1915, seated in front of the shed. During the First World War three
women tram drivers and a conductress were employed. The figure seated at the centre front
is the inspector. In addition to the motormen and conductors a secretary, blacksmith,
carpenter, cleaner, electrician, painter and mechanical fitter were employed.

POST OFFICE LOOP in North Street. The tramway feeder cable joined the system just beyond this point. This brought the electricity to the line from the Corporation's power-station opposite St James's Church. The station generated a direct current supply of 550 volts specially for the tramway.

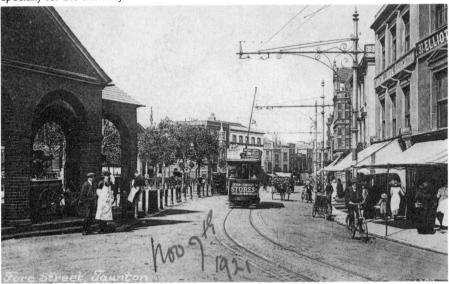

A TRAM IN FORE STREET, C. 1920. To improve the company's finances side advertisement boards were erected on the roofs and, subsequently, diagonally across and surrounding the headlamps. Ultimately adverts obliterated all dash numerals, but the crews could recognize individual cars at a glance.

# The Railway

GWR STATION, TAUNTON. The first decade of the century was the heyday of the family rail excursion. On August Bank Holiday 1910 trains took 900 Tauntonians to Weston-Super-Mare, 850 to Watchet and 650 to Minehead. Another 180 set off for Dawlish, Teignmouth and Torquay.

INTERIOR OF TAUNTON STATION, C. 1905, showing the platforms and overall roof. (E. Poteau)

HOLT TRACTOR AND HOWITZER at Taunton Station 1915. The writer of this card states, 'Leaving here for Southampton in the morning. This is one of the caterpillars which draws the guns. They are funny looking machines and a better name could not be found for them.' (M. Cooper)

TAUNTON STATION, EAST SIDE, C. 1905. To the right is East Station box and beyond this the water-tower. Three tracks carried through traffic into the station, while tracks to the left led to the goods shed and the west loop to the locomotive depot. At the end of the Second World War a locomotive was accidentally driven off the depot turntable and through the wall to overhang Station Road. (I've never seen a photograph of this, though – Author).

LAST BROAD-GAUGE TRAIN at Taunton 20 May 1892. These Gooch 422 8ft singles were a classic broad-gauge design. Prior to the conversion of gauge a similar engine had achieved a speed of 81 mph down the Wellington bank.

GWR 3066 *DUCHESS OF ALBANY*, at Taunton Station. This locomotive, one of the popular 422 class, was built in 1897 and ran until 1913. (E. Poteau)

SADDLE TANK ENGINE awaiting departure from the Barnstaple bay at Taunton Station.

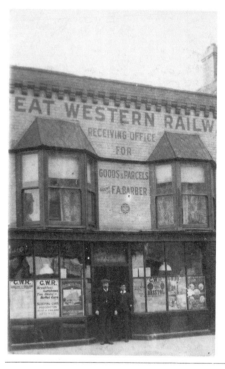

GWR PARCEL OFFICE, High Street, c. 1912, run by Mr F.A. Barber. He was a well-known booking-agent in the town who organized many rail excursions for Taunton people before the First World War. (Return London fare 6s. 6d. in 1914).

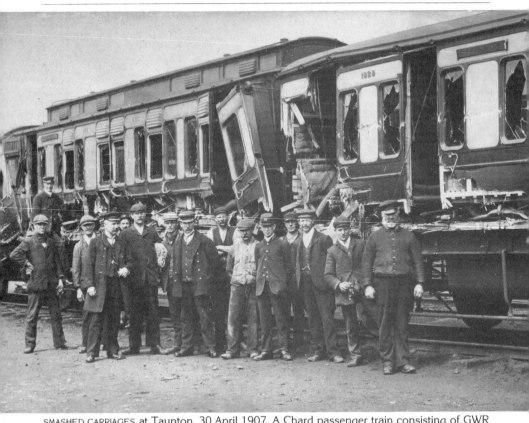

SMASHED CARRIAGES at Taunton, 30 April 1907. A Chard passenger train consisting of GWR engine 537 and four coaches was struck by an Exeter goods locomotive shunting at Obridge. Seven passengers were injured and the goods locomotive derailed and badly damaged. Three of the passenger coaches were wrecked. Postcards of the accident were in the post before the end of the same day.

AFTER THE COLLISION at Obridge in 1907 engine 537 at Taunton shed. The locomotive was an 042 tank built in 1868. She was repaired and kept in service until 1932. The bearded gentleman is probably her driver, Mr F. Oram of Chard.

THE HULK OF LOCOMOTIVE KING GEORGE VI at Taunton Shed 1940. This locomotive drawing 13 carriages ran off the relief line at Norton Fitzwarren. There were 27 passengers killed and 56 seriously injured. (Full story and photographs due in *Around Taunton in Old Photographs*.)

TAUNTON GWR STATION from the air, c. 1927. Originally built as a one sided design (i.e. virtually two separate stations serving the up and down lines) the station opened in 1842. The Bristol and Exeter Company replaced this layout with a larger 'single' station and added an all over roof in 1868. In 1895 the GWR considerably extended the platforms. Major rebuilding started in 1930 and by 1932 the all over roof had been removed. In this view the goods shed and office are bottom left. (Photochrom Co.)

# People and Events

WILLIAM HENRY ASKWITH, Archdeacon of Taunton and Vicar of St Mary's Church for 23 years. He died on 9 April 1911 aged 67. (Abraham)

MR ASKWITH'S COFFIN enters St Mary's Church for the funeral service. The coffin had been made by the Archdeacon's precentor Mr T. Doble. (M. Cooper)

THE HEARSE DEPARTS for the funeral procession. The shops in the town closed between 11.30 a.m. and 1.30 p.m. as a mark of respect. Shortly after Askwith's death a memorial school was built off South Street. (The author being a former pupil.) (M. Cooper)

ASKWITH'S FUNERAL PROCESSION passes St John's Church 1911. The order of procession was as follows: 'the choir, churchwardens, the clergy, clergy pallbearers, chief mourners, the Mayor and Corporation, the Borough Magistrates, the Market Trustees, the Governors, teachers and pupils of Huish and Bishops Fox's Schools, etc. (M. Cooper)

TRAFALGAR DAY MILITARY PARADE in Vivary Park 1915. (M. Cooper)

PROCLAMATION OF KING GEORGE V at the Market House, May 1910. (M. Cooper)

THE DUKE OF YORK passing the Corn Exchange on his official visit to Taunton in 1922. The Duke was driven through the town in a 19 hp Crossley, supplied by the Taunton Motor Company. A kitten was dropped from a window into the Duke's lap and passed to a girl in the crowd. She called it Prince. (M. Cooper)

THE DUKE TAKING THE SALUTE at the Municipal Buildings. In the doorway stands the Mayor, Councillor F.S. Dodson. (M. Cooper)

THE DUKE OF YORK and senior members of the Somerset Light Infantry at the castle. The Duke had visited Taunton as Colonel in Chief of the SLI. (M. Cooper)

KING GEORGE VI AT TAUNTON STATION, 2 December 1937. The King passed through the town on a tour of the Duchy of Cornwall. He was received by the Lord Lieutenant of Somerset, the Marquis of Bath, who presented him to officers of the SLI Depot. Here he is about to inspect representatives of the Old Comrades Association in the station car park.

SIR ALEXANDER ACLAND HOOD'S election victory over Mr King declared at the Shire Hall. Sir A.A. Hood was MP for West Somerset from 1892–1911. (H.H. Hole)

SIR A.A. HOOD'S ELECTION VICTORY SPEECH on the portico of the Castle Hotel. (H.H. Hole)

MR HOPE SIMPSON being acclaimed Liberal MP for Taunton at the Municipal Buildings 1922.

NURSES BEING RECEIVED BY THE MAYOR, F.S. DODSON at the Municipal Buildings in 1922. (M. Cooper)

TAUNTON RED CROSS HOSPITAL, 1917, situated at Priory School. On 7 February 1916 the first convoy of wounded arrived and in the first year the hospital treated nearly 400 patients. Regular concerts were held to entertain the sick and wounded soldiers. (M. Cooper)

(Part) Taunton Division.

PART OF TAUNTON DIVISION POLICE FORCE, c. 1906. In 1884 the Taunton Division consisted of 27 constables, 2 serjeants and a superintendant.

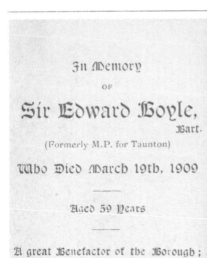

In Memory

OF

## Sir Edward Boyle,

Bart.

(Formerly M.P. for Taunton)

Who Died March 19th, 1909

Aged 59 Years

A great Benefactor of the Borough;
endeared and loved by all.

MOURNING CARD FOR SIR EDWARD BOYLE 1909. Sir Edward was elected MP for Taunton in the General Election of 1906. He retired as MP shortly before his death. (M. Cooper)

FRANK WILLIAM PRITCHETT BROWN born 1867, Mayor of Taunton 1923–24. Mr Pritchett Brown was a draper and manufacturer (of Clements and Brown) and one-time president of the Taunton Traders' Association. (J. Chaffin)

TAUNTON POLICE FORCE line up in front of the police station to celebrate Queen Victoria's Jubilee in either 1887 or 1897.

A FIRST WORLD WAR HOWITZER passes over the Tone Bridge c. 1915. Other photographs have suggested that these scenes were not uncommon in Taunton during the First World War. The children appear to be having fun running behind the heavy traction engine wheels. (M. Cooper)

THE JOYFUL SCENES on the Parade for Queen Victoria's 1897 Diamond Jubilee. The festivities also included a dinner for 700 over sixties in the Corn Exchange and Municipal Hall. In the lower left-hand corner an ice-cream vendor has just sold ice-creams to two children.

THE PARADE DECORATED for the 1897 Jubilee. After celebrations on the Parade a public luncheon was held in Vivary Park. Another photograph in this series shows the large marquee in which the event took place.

MR VAN TRUMP AND HIS STAFF'S CARNIVAL FLOAT outside the St Augustine Street works which were built in 1898. Mr Van Trump was proprietor of the Tone Vale Manufacturing Company and Mayor of Taunton during the First World War. Mr Van Trump's son Harry survived an aeroplane crash over the sea with Henri Salmet the French Aviator in 1914, only to be killed in action in 1916. Van Trump also lost a nephew in the war. (E. Cox)

THE TONE VALE MANUFACTURING COMPANY proudly display their first prize card after entering Taunton Carnival in 1907.

ANOTHER SUCCESSFUL YEAR FOR VAN TRUMP and his staff in the carnival of 1908. (Mr Van Trump is second from the left.) (E.E. Cox)

TONE VALE MANUFACTURING COMPANY'S 'Italian Singers'. Taunton's first modern carnival took place in 1891 in aid of the hospital. This continued nearly every year until the First World War. (M. Cooper)

ANOTHER YEAR'S CARNIVAL ENTRY at St Augustine Street. The Carnival was revived in 1922 and ran until 1929. Further carnivals were seen between 1933 and the Second World War. Although a carnival took place in 1953 for the coronation, the current revival started only in 1966.

*Victorian Era, Taunton Manfg C̄o Taunton & Rowbarton Carnival 28·9·22*

POOL WALL MILL'S STAFF in the Taunton Carnival 28 February 1922. This is one of six floats entered by this factory which showed the changing fashions in costume between 1837 and 1887 (presumably this postcard is one of a set of six by W.A. Crockett).

CHILDREN IN CARNIVAL DRESS, c. 1909, outside the Albemarle Baptist Chapel which opened in 1875. (E.E. Cox)

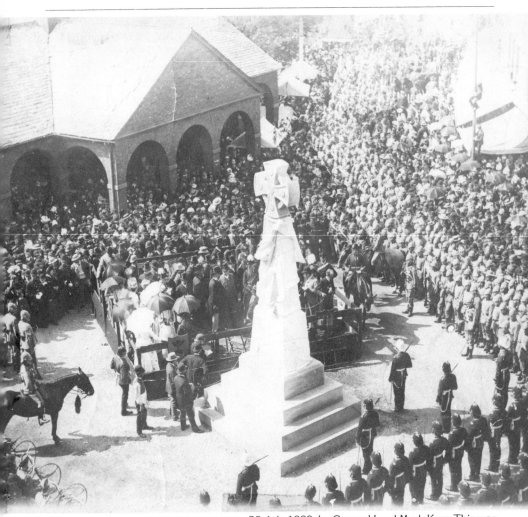

UNVEILING OF THE BURMESE WAR MEMORIAL, 30 July 1889, by General Lord Mark Kerr. This was erected to commemorate men of the Somerset Light Infantry killed in the third Burmese War of 1885–1887.

# Pubs and Hotels

'GOOD CIDER' IS ON SALE at Thomas Reeves' Robin Hood Inn c. 1907. This public house was situated in Somerset Place at the bottom of Alfred Street and held by Mr Reeves from March 1906 to November 1908.

MICHAEL CLARKE AND HIS WIFE outside their Somerset Inn, Alfred Street. Mr Clarke held the pub between c. 1904 and 1912. At this time there were two Somerset Inns in the town (see page 108).

THE COMPASS INN, c. 1905, at the top of Cann Street. The inn, originally known as the Square and Compasses (1768) was known at the Compass Inn from 1711. Starkey, Knight and Ford held the premises as the Compass Hotel until its demolition in around 1963.

THE GEORGE INN, at the junction of Staplegrove Road and Station Road c. 1907. The inn and the Flook House wall were removed in June 1907. On the lamp-post in the foreground, are an emergency fire escape ladder and telephone fire-alarm. (E. Cox)

THE CASTLE HOTEL, C. 1930, at this time three storeys high. The fourth storey was added in 1965.

CASTLE HOTEL LOUNGE BAR C. 1930.

CASTLE HOTEL, ENTRANCE HALL, c. 1930.

CASTLE HOTEL, THE LOUNGE, c. 1930.

THE OLD ANGEL, Corporation Street, here c. 1925, was recorded as early as 1688. The inn was renamed The Sportsman's Inn in 1956 and was later demolished. The National bus and charabanc booking office is on the right.

E HART HOTEL c. 1862. One of Taunton's most notorious inns is situated on the High Street. By 1865 it had been converted to Myer Jacobs Furnishing Warehouse 16) later to be the Devon and Somerset Stores. (E. Goodman)

Castle Hotel.

THE CASTLE HOTEL c. 1902. Originally separate from Clarke's Hotel (below) but united in 1928 by Harrison's Hotels Limited who owned both premises. The corner section was taken over by Burtons whose foundation stone was laid in 1929.
(M. Cooper)

CHARLES NATION'S CLARKE'S HOTEL c. 1900. Built originally as a private house for the Easton family c. 1815, it first opened as an hotel in 1834. From April 1888 until his bankruptcy in February 1901 the hotel was held by C.J. Nation.

# WHITTINGHAM'S LONDON HOTEL TAUNTON.

LARGE ASSEMBLY HALL FOR BANQUETS
BALLS AND THEATRICALS
TELEPHONE. 134.

WHITTINGHAM'S LONDON HOTEL, advertising postcard, c. 1914. Originally known as the Three Cups, the hotel is the oldest recorded public house in Taunton (1528). Many distinguished personalities have visited the hotel including: John Wesley, General Booth, Winston Churchill and Queen Elizabeth II. Walter Whittingham, a local wine and spirit merchant, acquired the hotel in 1913 from Ernest Claridge. After Whittingham's death in 1919 his widow sold out to Trust Houses Limited who renamed the hotel the County Hotel. (M. Cooper)

The London Hotel, Taunton.     70871 J.V

CLARIDGE'S LONDON HOTEL, c. 1912. Bristolian Ernest Claridge took over the hotel in 1901. In this photograph the horse bus Claridge introduced in 1903 can be seen. In 1914 it was said that 'In bad weather the horsed bus is a trial to the temper of the passengers and a strain on the animals especially where tram rails have to be traversed.' The photograph also shows placards for Poole's Pictures in the Empire Cinema, a West Somerset Dairy milk cart and Hook's enormous teapot on the wall of their shop at Cheapside. (Valentine XL)

THE SOMERSET INN, Upper High Street, c. 1908, run by Alfred Jennings (1902–1926). In the picture is Mr Baker in his butcher's apron and a policeman from the station across the road.

BRIDGE STREET, c. 1915, showing the Myrtle Tree and Black Horse Hotel (right).

# Frost, Flood and Fire

MR JABEZ HARRIS, CONFECTIONER of No. 25 East Street set up an igloo stall at the base of the Kingslake Memorial during the great blizzard of 1881. (Petherick)

SKATING ON THE RIVER TONE, January 1881. After snow on 12 January a blizzard of snow and gale force winds began on Monday 17 January. The storm did not ease until Wednesday evening. At the height of the storm even the skaters did not venture forth. (Petherick)

EAST STREET AFTER THE BLIZZARD OF JANUARY 1881. Clearance work achieved little until Saturday 29 January when 230 men and boys worked on the streets. Free passage was not finally possible until the following Monday. (Petherick)

THE TONE BRIDGE withstands the floods of October 1960. Masses of timber from the timber yard had swept against the bridge supports. There was genuine fear, for a while, that the bridge would collapse.

BRIDGE STREET DURING THE FLOODS of October 1960. The author remembers well wading through the flooded streets as a child. At the junction of Staplegrove Road we all had to hold hands to cross the road as the current was so strong.

FIRE AT STONE'S GARAGE, TAUNTON. DEC 31/07.

FIRE AT STONE'S GARAGE 1907. The fire occurred on 31 December at Mr Stone's Garage and Cycle Depot at Staplegrove Road. It can be seen from the photograph that at least three motor cars were wrecked in the blaze. Mr Stone would have had only a short dash to reach the emergency fire depot on the lamp-post opposite his shop (see page 101).

# Social, Sports and Leisure

VIVARY PARK, c. 1915, bought by the borough from Dr Kinglake in 1893. The bandstand was erected two years later. (E. Gill)

THE CORN EXCHANGE, left, housed the Exchange Electric Theatre better known to Tauntonians as the 'Bug House'. The town's first cinema opened as the Picturedrome here in 1910. (Knight)

THE EMPIRE ELECTRIC THEATRE was opened in September 1910 in the London Hotel Assembly Rooms. The proprietor was Mr C. Poole of Poole's Myriorama, a former Tauntonian who had become famous for his picture houses. The hotel and cinema placards are pictured here, post 1919, after the name was changed to the County Hotel. (W.H.S. Kingsway)

Bridge Street, Taunton.

THE LYCEUM was built on the site of the Old George Inn. Spiller and Browne commenced work on the building in March 1913 having secured the contract for £3,500. The Cinema opened on 18 August 1913. (A.K. Baker)

THE CINEMA IN THE LONDON HOTEL survived as the County Cinema until its closure in 1934. At the time of this photograph in 1932 George Vickery was the lessee. (Lilywhite)

THE GAUMONT CINEMA shortly after its opening in 1932. The plans for this 'super cinema' were unveiled in the *Gazette* of 17 May 1930. (Frith)

TAUNTON CASTLE has its origins in the twelfth century. The Somerset Archaeological and Natural History Society purchased it in 1874 and it is here that the Society's extensive collection of exhibits and books are stored. (M. Cooper)

THE WESTERN END OF THE CASTLE GREAT HALL soon after its re-opening as a museum by the SANHS in 1902.

GREAT HALL TAUNTON CASTLE MUSEUM,
HERE JUDGE JEFFREYS HELD HIS BLOODY ASSIZE

THE GREAT HALL showing museum exhibits as they were laid out c. 1903. (E.A.S.)

DELLER'S CAFE situated by the Tone Bridge was a popular meeting place between the wars. (E. Goodman)

DELLER'S CAFE INTERIOR, C. 1923. The main cafe was on the ground and first floors, it was open for 12 hours daily. (E. Goodman)

DELLER'S CAFE FIRST FLOOR, c. 1923. The first floor had an orchestra gallery and the top floor was arranged as a dance and supper room. (E. Goodman)

DELLER'S CAFE FIRST FLOOR, c. 1923. A different view of the grand central staircase showing what a fine and spacious cafe this was. Some of the plaster moulding still survives behind subsequent modifications to the building. (E. Goodman)

TAUNTON RUGBY FOOTBALL CLUB FIRST XI 1904–5. Back row, left to right: Frank Larway (sec.), R. Govier, H. Woodman, H.H. Ford, C.W. Bennett, P.J. Barnicott, W.M. Penny, P. Browne (Treas.), W. Churchill, J. Hammacott, C.S. Northcote, A. Gregory, B. Hughes, W.J. Vickery, H. Winter, H. Bond and J. Larcombe.

TAUNTON RUGBY FOOTBALL CLUB RESERVES 1904–5. Back row, left to right: W.G. Edwards (ref.), H. Hughes, T. Horrill, F. Hurford, H.W. Rowsell, W.G. Vickery, J. Hammacott, J.C. Bragg (sec.), Revd H.F. Elgood, J. Mapledoram, E. Ware, G.H. Darling (Capt.), F. Poole, W. Baker, J. Baker, Z. Sims, W. Pike.

TAUNTON COUNTY CRICKET GROUND c. 1902. The Somerset players were granted first class status in 1891. The club has had an eventful history and their greatest triumph was in 1979 when the Gillette Cup and John Player League were won in one glorious weekend. (Tuck)

TAUNTON VALE FOXHOUNDS meet at the Castle Hotel in January 1934. The hunt had its kennels at Henlade. (Photochrom Co.)

THE ROLLER-SKATING RINK, Wellington Road, c. 1911. The proprietors, Taunton Skating Rinks Limited of No. 4 The Bridge, opened the rink in 1911. This coincided with Britain's second roller-skating boom, the sport being known as 'rinking'. The first roller-skate patent was taken out by American, James Plympton in 1863 and the sport was at its most popular in Britain between the years 1870–75, 1908–12 and 1948–54. (M. Cooper)

# SECTION TEN

# Buildings

Municipal Buildings, Taunton

THE MUNICIPAL BUILDINGS in Corporation Street, originally erected as the town's grammar school in 1522 by Bishop Richard Fox. The street runs where the castle moat used to be and the buildings are on the higher ground that used to form part of the castle's outer defences.

THE TECHNICAL INSTITUTE was opened in February 1900 by the Mayor W.A. Wrenn and his principal guest Professor Silvanus Thompson. Students had access to lecture and classrooms, and laboratories for electrical, physical and mechanical work. (Valentine)

THE PUBLIC LIBRARY opened in 1905. Mr Andrew Carnegie contributed £5,000 towards the £7,000 cost of the building, which was built by T.H. Moggridge. (Stengal)

THE SCHOOL OF ART was opened in 1907. Its departments originally included metal working, casting, modelling and painting rooms etc. (Now Headquarters of Taunton Area Social Services Department). (M. Cooper)

THE SHIRE HALL was home to the Assize and Quarter Sessions. It was built between 1855 and 1858. The six inch bore, twenty-four pounder cannon, a Crimean War relic, was given to the town by the government in 1857. (Wykham)

CASTLE GREEN, c. 1786. This view is from the probable west gate of the outer castle ward, looking towards Castle Bow and the East Gate. In the early sixteenth century this entire area would have been surrounded by a moat. (Goodman)

THE INNER WARD of Taunton Castle c. 1905. The Grand Jury and Witness Room (on pillars) was added in around 1790 and demolished in 1931. (Knight)

THE PRISON C. 1902. A prison was first erected on this site in 1754 and greatly enlarged in 1815. The last public hanging here was of George Britton who was executed in 1867 for the murder of his wife at Woolverton near Frome. Executions continued inside the prison for a few more years but were eventually transferred to Shepton Mallet. The prison itself was closed in 1884. The Territorial Army moved into the building in 1913 but all that now remains of it are the central tower and the block to the left. (Abraham)

ST MARGARET'S 'LEPER' HOSPITAL c. 1902. A leper hospital had probably existed on this site as early as c. 1180. The present building dates from the early sixteenth century. It had been converted to an almshouse by 1612. (Abraham)

ST JAMES' STREET ALMSHOUSES, built c. 1500 and demolished in 1897. Hanbury and Cotchin took over the site to extend their Canon Street Brewery. One bay survives in the grounds of Taunton Castle. (Published as a postcard by Brice c. 1902)

POPE'S AND GRAY'S ALMSHOUSES, East Street, c. 1905. Pope's Almshouses were demolished in 1933. The two shops between were H.J. Rowe fruiterers and A.W. Lee's shaving salon.

THE PRIORY 'BARN' c. 1902. A rare surviving medieval building in Taunton, the sole remains of Taunton Priory. Believed to be one wing of a gatehouse, the actual use is unknown. The building is now a cricket museum.

THE POST OFFICE, CHURCH SQUARE, c. 1906. At this time there were 32 postmen in the town operating five deliveries daily (except Thursday which had four and Sunday one only). (Brice)

THE NEW POST OFFICE, NORTH STREET, opened 19 March 1911 having been built by Pollard and Son of Bridgwater for £7,000 on the site of the old Spread Eagle Inn. The clock was added in May the same year by public subscription. (E.A.S.)

THE SOMERSET SAVINGS BANK, Upper High Street. This postcard celebrated the Bank's centenary on 6 September 1917. Formed in North Street the bank removed to this site (the old Full Moon Inn) in 1831. The building has now been converted to apartments.

FLOOK HOUSE, Station Road, c. 1902. At this time occupied by Miss Sibly and her Ladies' Collegiate School. The former extensive grounds now contain the swimming pool and new Borough Council offices. (Abraham)

JELLALABAD BARRACKS, c. 1902, former home of the Somerset Light Infantry, they were completed in 1880. (Abraham)

THE OLD POLICE STATION, SHUTTERN, c. 1904. It was built in 1857 to house the Taunton Division force. An extension was built in 1874 to accommodate several single men, the building was finally demolished in 1963.

GENERAL VIEW OF TAUNTON, c. 1900, from the Tower of St George's Church. In the centre is Billet Street now no longer a throughfare into East Street. The bottom right-hand corner has been extensively redeveloped. The towers of St Mary's and St James' dominate the skyline. (M. Cooper)

GENERAL VIEW OF TAUNTON from an aeroplane in the late 1920s. Most noticeable is the dense cluster of buildings off High Street and North Street, many of which formed the old courts of Taunton. The demolition of these areas provided the open spaces used for car-parks today. (Aerofilms)

# SECTION ELEVEN

# Along the River

VIEW TOWARDS TAUNTON and the cricket ground from Priory Fields, c. 1902.

ENCH WEIR TAUNTON.

THE OLD PENSTOCK AND WEIR at French Weir, c. 1910. The horse-chestnut trees were planted in 1898 and the first swings were erected five years later. In 1914–15 the weir was completely rebuilt, the work being seriously disrupted during flooding on 20 July 1914. The island downstream of the weir was removed during the flood prevention scheme in 1967. A story the author remembers well concerns a drunk who fell into the river and after struggling manfully to the bank found, to his dismay, that he was on the island and had to repeat the process all over again. (E.A.S.)

FRENCH WEIR, C. 1910, showing an uninterrupted view across the fields to St John's Church. (W.H.S. Kingsway)

THE NEW WEIR AND BRIDGE at French Weir, C. 1915. (Frith)

The French Weir, Taunton.

CHILDREN IN THE TONE at French Weir, c. 1905. The end of Portland Street and Clarence Street are in the distance. (Senior)

VIEW FROM TONE BRIDGE, c. 1920 with the Taunton Brewery, now Goodlands Gardens, on the left. The brewery was demolished in 1958 and the gardens formed in 1971 in memory of Alderman William Goodland (Mayor 1898–99).

AERIAL VIEW OF THE RIVER and Tone Bridge taken in the late 1920s. This view of the river stretches from the cricket ground (left) to the old town mills beyond the Taunton Brewery. Many of the industrial buildings in this area have now been cleared. The Brewhouse Theatre stands on the site of the West Somerset Brewery bought by S.W. Arnold and Sons in 1897 and partially demolished in 1903. Thomas Starkey of North Petherton bought the Taunton Brewery in 1881 and the firm Starkey Knight and Ford ran it from 1895 until the brewery's closure in the 1950s. (Aerofilms)

STONE ARCH BRIDGE over the Tone, c. 1893. Harry Frier, the artist used this very same photograph to paint two watercolours of the old bridge. In Harry's version the left-hand arch (a remnant of the older bridge partially rebuilt in 1834) is inaccurately shown. During the 1834 rebuilding of the central arches a stone bottle was sealed in the masonry with a note stating — 'This centre arch was erected at the expense of the Taunton and Bridgwater Canal Company and the first stone was laid on Thursday the 29th May in the year of our Lord 1834.'

THE TONE BRIDGE prior to its partial rebuilding in 1834. St James' church tower is in the centre of the picture.

THE NEW TONE BRIDGE; a photograph possibly taken at the time of the 1902 coronation as Bridge Street is decorated with flags. The bridge was built in 1894 at a cost of £7,000 from a design by J.H. Smith the Borough Surveyor. (Brice)

FRENCH WEIR BATHING STATION, C. 1915. A bathing place was established at French Weir in 1862. Bathing times were arranged so that no mixed bathing took place. (Valentine)

THE MILL STREAM through Tangier, C. 1902. The sheds in the centre are part of the old Tangier Brewery run by the Oram family from 1855–1879. The last surviving member of the family in brewing at Taunton was Edward who managed the Taunton Brewery in the early 1900s.

A VIEW OF THE GASWORKS from the French Weir before the demolition of the gasholders. It would appear that the coking plant is still in the course of construction.

THE FIREPOOL LOCKS, c. 1915, with Van Trump's collar factory and Canon Street Brewery chimney in the distance. (H.M. Jones)

STEAM LAUNCH AND LIMEKILNS at Firepool c. 1900. The Bridgwater and Taunton Canal was opened to as far as Huntworth in 1827. The connection with Bridgwater was not finally achieved until 1841. In 1867 the Great Western Railway bought the canal whose trade, in competition with the railway, slowly declined until the last commercial barge ran in 1907. Unlike its neighbours the Grand Western and Chard canals, the Bridgwater and Taunton canal remains open throughout its original length.

# Religion and Education

ST MARY'S CHURCH from Hammet Street, c. 1910. The original tower became unsafe and was rebuilt between 1858 and 1862 from Williton stone given by Sir A. Hood. (W.H.S.)

ST ANDREW'S CHURCH, here C. 1902, was completed in 1881 at a cost of £2,500. The church was substantially enlarged in 1893 at a cost of £5,000, the work being carried out by H.J. Spiller the original builder. (Frith)

ST JOHN'S CHURCH, C. 1910, designed by Sir Gilbert Scott.

THE TEMPLE WESLEYAN CHURCH, Upper High Street, c. 1902, was built in 1808 on land purchased by James Lackington, a famous London bookseller born at Wellington. The Wesleyan Methodists were given use of the chapel in 1811. (Valentine)

ST JAMES' CHURCH c. 1902. The tower of this church was completely rebuilt shortly after the completion of St Mary's tower. (Valentine)

THE FRANCISCAN CONVENT C. 1902. Built originally in 1772 for use as a hospital, the building was converted to a convent in 1808. In this view, from the tower of St Georges, Gwynne Lane is in the foreground. Also shown is the farmhouse (built 1868) and vegetable garden. Most Tauntonians will remember the building as St Joseph's Convent School from 1954 to 1978. The premises and grounds now form part of King's College. (M. Cooper)

THE CONVENT from the playground, c. 1903.

THE CONVENT ORATORY c. 1903. The oratory chapel was originally furnished in 1875. These two views are from a set of at least ten postcards of the convent by the Photo Tourists Association.

# QUEEN'S COLLEGE, TAUNTON,
## SPEECH DAY, OCTOBER 16th, 1908.

Mr. Arthur Henderson, M.P.     A. S. Haslam, Esq., M.A.     W. H. Reed, Esq., J.P.     Henry Holloway, Esq.J.P. Alderman J. P. Sill
(Head Master).     Mrs. W. H. Reed.
Lewis Williams, Esq., J.P. (Chairman of Directors).     Mrs. Arthur Henderson.
The Mayor of Taunton     The Mayoress.     Sir Robert Hart.     Lady Hart.     Rev. D. J. Waller, D.D.
(Alderman A. J. Spiller).

NER, Photographer.

SPEECH DAY AT QUEEN'S COLLEGE 1908. The college was established in 1843 and reorganised and renamed in 1888. This particular speech day was a special occasion for the college. Sir Robert Hart, GCMG Inspector General of Chinese Customs and Posts, a former pupil of the school and 'financial pilot of the Chinese Empire' had agreed to present the prizes. Lady Hart also opened the new college swimming pool. During his visit to Taunton Sir Robert was made an Honorary Freeman of the Borough. The charter was presented in a special casket featuring views of Queen's College, the Municipal Buildings, Taunton Castle and Vivary Park.

THE TEMPLE INTERIOR C. 1902. (Abraham)

SILVER STREET BAPTISTS' SUNDAY SCHOOL handbell ringers. A photograph possibly taken around the time of the school's centenary in 1915.

BISHOP FOX'S SCHOOL, Staplegrove Road. These buildings were erected in 1904 and considerably enlarged in 1907. This photograph was taken by M. Cooper in around 1905.

BISHOP FOX'S SCHOOL, the art room, c. 1918. The school had originally opened in the Crescent in 1890. (Buchanan)

ishop Fox's Girls' School, Taunton. ——— Housecraft Room

HOUSECRAFT ROOM, Bishop Fox's School, c. 1918. The school had six classrooms, a cookery lecture room and kitchen, an art room, chemical laboratory and lecture room, cloak rooms and head and assistant mistresses' rooms. Attached to the school were model gardens, lawn tennis and basketball courts and playing fields. There was also a hostel for boarders. The premises are now a branch of the Somerset College for Arts and Technology. (Buchanan)

THE LABORATORY, Bishop Fox's School, c. 1918. The school moved to Kingston Road in 1940.

TAUNTON GIRLS' SCHOOL, c. 1925, opened originally in January 1922 as the Park Street School for girls at No. 12 Park Street. Mrs Rapp the principal moved into St Mary's Vicarage in May 1922 and renamed the school the Taunton Modern School for Girls. (Buchanan)

TAUNTON GIRLS' SCHOOL MOTOR CAR, c. 1925, with which a collection service for pupils was offered. The school had approximately 46 girl pupils, 7 boys of kindergarten age and 4 staff.

TAUNTON GIRLS' SCHOOL, the homely surroundings inside the old vicarage, c. 1925. The tenancy of this building was short lived for, by 1930, Mrs Rapp had moved the school to Burnham-On-Sea after another spell at Park Street.

unton School.
e Gymnasium.

THE GYMNASIUM, Taunton School, c. 1905. The school originally opened in 1847 on the Wellington Road but moved to new premises off Staplegrove Road in 1870. The gymnasium sports an array of unsophisticated apparatus designed to improve the physical well-being of the young pupils. (M. Cooper)

TAUNTON SCHOOL c. 1902. The main building was constructed of grey Westleigh stone with Bath stone facings. (Stengel)

unton School. Headmaster's House and Master's Boarding House.

TAUNTON SCHOOL, Headmaster's House and Master's Boarding House for boys aged 10½ to 14 years. (M. Cooper)

TAUNTON SCHOOL, Foxcombe Dormitory 1917, situated on Greenway Road.

Taunton School.
Athletic and Day Dressing Rooms-
Shower Bath.

TAUNTON SCHOOL ATHLETIC AND DAY DRESSING ROOMS and shower bath, c. 1905. In the 1930s the school catered for 600 boys, 400 of whom were boarders. (M. Cooper)

TAUNTON SCHOOL, HEADMASTER'S HOUSE DINING ROOM, c. 1905. (M. Cooper)

TAUNTON SCHOOL, FIVES COURTS AND SWIMMING BATHS, c. 1905. The sporting facilities offered by the school included 50 acres of playing fields with tennis courts and a running track. (M. Cooper)

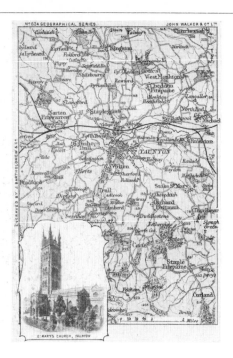

ST. MARY'S CHURCH, TAUNTON

## ACKNOWLEDGEMENTS

The following people have kindly allowed the author to copy several of the photographs appearing in this book: Mrs J. Comer, Miss Baker, Mrs K. Handell, Wendy Waghorn, Mr J. Laverock and Mrs D. Chedzoy. A debt of gratitude for information and assistance is due to: Sally-Anne Chipchase (typing), Robin Bush (for corrections and additions to my preliminary copy), David Bromwich (research at Local History Library) and the late Mrs Paradine (née Philips) for information regarding H.M. Cooper.

All facts in this book have been checked as carefully as possible. However, memories fade and original sources can contain errors. If readers can supply additional information or lend original photographs for copying I hope they will contact me.

DEDICATION

I should like to dedicate this book to my family, Liz, Vicky and Jonathan.